Who Was Steve Jobs?

The Legacy of the Tech Titan

The Story of a Boy Who's Love for Tinkering With Electronics Resulted in the Invention of the First Apple Machine.

By Phil Cooper

"Love yourself and what you do – The only key to success."

— Steve Jobs

Who Was Steve Jobs?

Steve Jobs… the MAN, the LEGEND, the Apple Founder… was a genius who gave the world access to technology that is still changing the world. To this day, his greatest accomplishment is the iPhone and still is.

Taken away too soon, his legacy still lives on. Countless entrepreneurs look up to him and use his advice to succeed in the business world. If it wasn't for him, we would have never been introduced to portable computers and mobile phones with touch screens.

Table of Contents

Introduction

Steve Jobs.

Does the name even need an introduction?

Today, the entire world is familiar with it. This name is so incredibly intimidating and inspiring that no one can measure up to it.

He's the man who created *Apple*.

He's the man who wore black turtlenecks and created a uniform of power with his simple attire.

He's the man who changed the face of technology forever.

The tech titan's ingenuity has left behind a legacy that, to this date, is unparalleled.

The name in itself is a brand that instantly inspires entrepreneurs who love technology to do more.

For Steve, life was a little easier than all those entrepreneurs who struggled in life due to personal problems. They say that reaching your goals does not seem hard when you grow up in a loving home. You have people surrounding you who encourage you to pursue your dreams, and if you think about it, that's all it takes to succeed.

We cannot downplay Steve's struggles. He missed out on something that he had no idea about. However, he still made it.

Like other heroes, Steve's journey had its fair share of downfalls and hardships. He stood strong through every fall and looked for an opportunity to learn from his mistakes and turn things around. This enabled him to create an industry that changed the course of the future.

One thing that no one can deny is that Steve was born a genius. His passion fueled the fire to accomplish his goals and achieve something new and unique that no one else had ever before.

Lo and behold, he was able to do this with Apple.

When America sought ways to maintain an innovative edge, Steve stood as the icon of applied imagination and inventiveness. He knew the only way to create value in the 21st century was to combine technology and creativity. Thus, a company was built where imagination was combined with extraordinary feats of engineering.

"The people who are crazy enough to think they can change the world are the ones who do."

— Apple's "Think Different" Commercial, 1997

With his most prized invention – Apple – Steve proved that no matter how crazy an idea might seem to you, the best way to find out whether it will be successful or not is to act on it.

Steve always encouraged people to speak honestly. Though he followed his own advice, he could sometimes be brutally honest, which confused people about his personality. His colleagues, friends, and foes gave an unvarnished look into his perfectionism, passions, obsessions, devilry, and artistry, with which he shaped his business that resulted in the innovative products we use today.

During some parts of his life, Steve found himself driven by demons that drove people around him to despair and fury. But his products and personality were interrelated, similar to Apple's software and hardware.

Steve's tale of success is cautionary and instructive, filled with lessons on leadership, values, character, and most important of all — *innovation*.

The Story of Steve Jobs

The story begins with adoption, which led to a happy life. Steve was born in San Francisco, California. His parents were two graduate students – Abdul Fattah Jandali (Syrian descent) and Joanne Carole Schieble (Swiss-German descent).

However, since his parents were just students, they decided to put him up for adoption as soon as he was born. Steve's parents were good people, and they wanted to make sure that he went to a loving, educated, wealthy family.

Fate has something else in store for Steve. He was adopted by Clara and Paul Jobs. The couple was loving but had no college education.

Paul was a coast guard in World War II. Soon after returning home, he married Clara within a few weeks. A few years later, he was deployed on the USS General M. C. Meigs. After the war had ended and Paul no longer wanted to work in the army, he and Clara decided to settle down.

Paul started working as a mechanic, while Clara stayed at home. The one thing that was missing from their lives was a baby. However, Clara has suffered an ectopic pregnancy and, after many complications, was told she would never be able to conceive again.

That's when they decided to adopt, and God rewarded them with a sweet baby boy.

When Steve turned 6, he found out he was adopted. Like any other child, Steve felt abandoned. Paul and Clara chose their words carefully to explain that he was wanted. That's when

Steve learned the meaning of Chosen and Special, and these two concepts became a part of his life.

The family faced some financial problems when Paul got transferred to Palo Alto as a repo man. So, he left the job and moved to Mountain View.

Steve's new life was full of surprises. Since his mother had already told him that he was adopted, he looked at the world with a different lens. After a work incident with his father, where he proved that the task at hand could be done his way, Steve realized that his parents understood who he really was — a genius.

His parents knew that Steve was special, and they wanted him to be treated that way at school. They saw that his potential was being wasted by memorizing trivial things, which weren't stimulating enough.

When Steve started 4th grade, he was put in an advanced class. His teacher would often bribe him with money and candy to read a book or solve complex math problems. After a while, the teacher no longer had to bribe him because all Steve wanted was to learn more. When he finished 4th grade, his teacher recommended that he should be tested. He scored at the high school sophomore level. Then, the school allowed Steve to jump two grades.

This jump proved to be disastrous for Steve. He was an awkward loner who had no friends. He was frequently bullied, and due to the violence in the neighborhood, he couldn't focus on his studies. Eventually, he insisted that his parents change his school. Money was tight at the time, and Jobs couldn't afford to make such a big change. However, when Steve told his parents that he would quit school if they didn't agree to his demand, they decided to buy a house in a new neighborhood.

The new house came with a garage, where Paul tinker with his cars and Steve with his electronics. There was a nice schooling district nearby, and the neighbors were extremely friendly.

Steve's parents wanted him to have a religious upbringing. They would take him to church every Sunday. This ended when Steve saw a magazine with a picture of starving children on it and questioned the pastor about it.

He asked the pastor, "Does God know about this?"

Steve didn't like the pastor's vague answer and announced that he couldn't worship a God who turned a blind eye to people's suffering.

Steve's dream of developing electronics came true in 9th grade. Larry Lang, his engineer neighbor who often invited Steve to his garage, got him interested in Heathkits. These assemble-it-yourself kits allowed Steve to develop electronic gear and radio.

Lang got him into the Hewlett-Packard Explorers Club. It was a club for students who loved engineering. The students would meet in the cafeteria, and an engineer from the company would tell them all about what he was working on. It was at HP that he first saw a desktop computer.

Students at the club were encouraged to do projects. Steve decided to make a frequency counter but didn't have some of the parts. So, he called HP's CEO and asked him for the parts. Not only did the CEO send him the parts, but he also gave him a job in the plant where frequency counters were made.

During one of his sophomore classes, he became friends with Stephen Wozniak, aka Steve, who also loved engineering. They both loved playing pranks on students and their teachers.

It was during one of these pranks that helped them create Apple.

Blue Box

It was 1971, and Steve Wozniak was about to drive off to his third college when he read an article in a magazine on *"Secrets of the Little Blue Box."*

The article described how phone breakers and hackers made free, long-distance phone calls by replicating the routed signal tones. He immediately called Steve and read long parts of the article on the phone. The Steves' made their way to the library to find a journal that listed all the frequencies.

After getting their hands on it, they went to an electronics shop and bought all the parts to make the analog tone operator. Using Steve's frequency counter, they calibrated the tones. When they tested their device, they didn't get the results they were hoping for.

The frequency counter wasn't what the device needed. Woz went back to Berkeley the next day and promised Steve he would work on a digital version of the frequency counter.

After making the digital part, Woz drove back to Steve's house, and they decided to try their device once again. They wanted to call Woz's uncle in Los Angeles but dialed the wrong number. It didn't matter, though, because the device worked.

Steve then made a prank call to the Vatican and asked to speak to the pope, posing as someone influential. Their invention was incredible! It was Steve who came up with the idea to sell their device. He calculated the cost of the components, which amounted to $40. They decided to sell the Blue Box for $150.

Dropping Out of College

In 1972, Steve enrolled in Reed College. The college was considered one of the most expensive ones in Oregon. Even though his parents couldn't afford the fee, they relented because Steve gave them an ultimatum that he wouldn't go to any other college.

Reed College had a hippie lifestyle but rigorous academic standards. Steve began experimenting with marijuana and psychedelic drugs. His time at college became more about discovering himself than studying.

At one point, Steve found himself out of cash and decided to sell his IBM Selectric typewriter. He walked into the room of the person who had wanted to buy it first and saw him and his girlfriend having sex. As he backed out of the room, Robert Friedland told him to take a seat. That was one of the most unreal experiences Steve had in life.

College didn't appeal to Steve. It's not that he didn't want to stay in college. He just thought that his parent's hard-earned money was being wasted on tuition. So, he decided to drop out.

When the dean of students heard what Steve was about to do, he gave him permission to audit classes and stay in a dorm room with his friends, even when he stopped paying the tuition fee.

The Start of a Beautiful Career – Atari

At the beginning of 1974, Steve moved back to his parent's house. He had spent 18 months on his college campus and, according to him, learned everything he wanted to.

He was now in search of a job. After looking at the *Classifieds* section in the newspapers, Steve found an opening at a video game manufacturing company called *Atari*.

Over the years, Steve's appearance had drastically changed. He had long, unkempt hair, which made him look like a hippie, he was on an all-fruit diet, which he believed reduced body odor (it didn't), and he was brash.

He walked into the Atari office and told Nolan Bushnell, the founder of the company, that he wouldn't leave until he was given a job.

Nolan's chief engineer Al Alcorn found Steve a bit odd, but his boss was intrigued, and so Steve was hired for $5 per hour. He was assigned to work with another engineer, who didn't like Steve much, especially because of his hygiene. Because of this, Steve started working the night shift.

Despite his unwillingness to work with other engineers and the fact that he played by his own rules, Steve produced many fun game designs.

The reason why Steve wanted to make money was that he also wanted to travel to India like Robert Friedland to find his guru.

One morning, he walked into Atari and announced he was leaving. Instead of questioning the weird turn of events, Alcorn wished him farewell. When Steve said he needed money for the journey, Alcorn said, "No."

During this time, the company was having trouble with its gaming kits in Munich. There was a problem with the interface that needed to be fixed. So Alcorn told Jobs to make a pit stop in Munich, fix the problem, and then fly to Dubai. Since all expenses were being paid by Atari, Steve agreed.

Steve explored New Delhi and Haridwar with Daniel Kottke (a friend from Reed College), met a Hindu Holy Man who shaved his head, and continued on the journey to finding himself.

When he arrived back in Oakland, his parents couldn't recognize him. Though he was back in his homeland, he still searched for like-minded people who were interested in Eastern spirituality, the search for enlightenment, Hinduism, and Zen Buddhism as much as him. For him, this was not a passing phase.

Stephen was still working at HP. When the January 1975 issue of Popular Mechanics arrived, the technology industry was abuzz with the news. Altair was introduced as the first computer kit that cost $495. Bill Gates got his hand on its first and started developing BASIC, a programming language. Steve and Stephen, too, got their hands on the kit. This was when the Homebrew Computer Club was born.

Stephen joined the first meeting held in the club, where he got to see the microprocessor. He had been working on a private project in HP, and with the microprocessor, he believed he would be able to create a standalone computer.

The idea was so appealing that Stephen started to sketch out the design, what would be later called Apple I. On Sunday, June 29, 1975, Stephen tested his design and couldn't believe his eyes when the screen displayed what he typed on the keyboard.

When Jobs learned about Stephen's success, he decided to get him the parts that would be needed to make the computer a complete success. Intel played a pivotal role in their journey when they gave them a few random-access memory chips for free on Steve's persuasion. Steve then started accompanying Stephen to the club.

By now, more engineers and technology enthusiasts had joined the club. The club had one rule, and that was to exchange ideas with fellow creators instead of commerce. When Bill Gates learned that his BASIC software was being shared with other people, he demanded this be stopped immediately. Steve was of the same mind and stopped Stephen from sharing his plans with other engineers.

His brilliant mind worked once again, and he decided to convince Stephen to sell the computers. Together, they came up with the initial investment and finally started their computer company.

Apple

Apple was initially born in 1976 with an agreement between Steve Jobs, Steve Wozniak, and Ron Wayne, Job's colleague at Atari. Jobs and Wozniak had a 45% stake in the partnership, and Ron had a 10% share. Even before the company went public, Ron got cold feet and ended his partnership. He sold his shares and received a total of $1,900 for them.

After their first demonstration at the club, they got an order from a computer shop. The owner agreed to pay $500 for each assembled computer, and the order was for 50 computers. A few months later, after working day and night on new projects, Stephen rolled out Apple II, a computer with a built-in keyboard.

On December 12, 1980, Apple went public, and all the employees who had options and stakes in the company became millionaires. Steve knew there was more to the computer world, and as history knows, he went on to create MacBook, iMac, iPhones, and iPads, along with the iOS system and iTunes.

Although the world got to know about Apple in 1980, it had already been making rounds in the technology world. By now, the company no longer held the appeal it once did when Steve introduced the first computer. Apple had lost 50% of its shares to IBM.

Steve wasn't impressed with the new turn of events. In 1984, he introduced the Apple Macintosh, which was one of his best creations of the time. However, not much was done for its marketing. Steve had planned to introduce it to the public as a standard computer for home, but it was too expensive. Not even the elite class was willing to pay $2,495 for it

Mac computers were later launched for businesses. It had little memory, no networking capabilities, and no hard drive. All in all, it had no useful features that corporate America could benefit from.

Steve's invention was failing right before his eyes, and he could do nothing about it. He was called in front of the board of directors to explain his error, but he had no answers. As a result, he was fired, and John Sculley replaced him as CEO, the person he had hired only a few days earlier.

Steve was stripped of all control and power. He decided to sell his Apple Stock and finally resigned in 1985.

With all the money he had made over the years and what he got after selling his stock, Steve started another company named Next Computers. These computers had fast processing speed, optical disk drive, and exceptional graphics. Despite such innovations, Steve wasn't able to attract the audience. For once, the computer was priced at a whopping $9,950, and second, it had no marketing potential.

After another failure, he set his sights on Pixar Animation Studio. He had bought it in 1986 from George Lucas, the founder of the company Lucas Film. Pixar was a subdivision of this company, which George had sold to Steve after a nasty divorce and the financial downfall of Lucas Film.

He struck a deal with Disney for three pictures, which turned out to be huge successes. He then took Pixar public, and after a few days of its arrival, Apple bought Next Computers for $400 million. Apple again appointed Steve, but this time, he was employed as an advisor to Gilbert F. Amelio, the CEO and Chairman of Apple.

iPhone – Apple's Most Prized Possession

The iPhone is perhaps the most famous device that Steve Jobs created. Now, sales of the device are major contributors to the company's revenue. Over the years, Apple has released a total of 34 iPhone variants, most of which have been received well by the public, except for a few that had battery problems.

On January 9, 2007, Steve revealed his best creation – iPhone, at a Macworld Conference. The phone offered many more features than an Android phone, which Steve explained to the audience for an hour.

When the first iPhone was introduced on June 29, 2007, the world got to hold the *King* of mobile phones. iPhone 1 measured 4.5 inches by 2.4 inches, had no 3rd party apps, and offered 16GB of flash memory. The phone was exclusive to the telecommunications company AT&T and ran on its unreliable and slow EDGE GSM network.

The iPhone debuted touchscreen as opposed to phones with a keypad, and the new interface got people hooked.

Many companies didn't believe that the iPhone would make a place in the market. These doubters were mostly CEOs, who were either threatened by the new invention or actually believed Steve couldn't accomplish something so life-changing.

Steve Ballmer, who was serving as the CEO of Microsoft at that time, said, *"There's no chance that the iPhone is going to get any significant market share."*

Jim Balsillie and Mike Lazaridis, who were serving as the CEOs of Blackberry at that time, watched in awe as Steve unveiled the iPhone. Mike couldn't believe his eyes and said,

"These people are really good," whereas Jim said, "We will be fine." We all know where Blackberry stands today, so you could say Jim was just consoling himself.

The launch of the first iPhone was just the beginning. Steve had always been the kind of person who wanted to do more. He knew that the iPhone would not be his last phone, so he set out to create different versions.

In July 2008, the next iPhone beat the previous version and became the successor. The 2nd generation device was called iPhone 3G, which had new hardware features, such as GPS, 3G data, and it was introduced at the Apple Store. This iPhone addressed two major drawbacks of the original version: its inability to access fast cellular-phone networks and cost. iPhone 3G showed a lot of promise and had the chance to become an excellent computing platform.

In June 2010, Verizon unveiled iPhone 4. This version of the iPhone had more advanced features, including a high resolution retina display, front camera, FaceTime, and multi-tasking functionality.

You are probably not interested in reading about the different versions of the iPhone. So, let's make this quick. In October 2011, the iPhone 4s was announced, introducing the public to Siri. Though Steve couldn't bask in the glory of his new invention, he did supervise iPhone 5's development, which hit the market in September 2012.

The founder of Apple had passed away, but his legacy lives on. Steve ensured that even after his demise, the world gets newer versions of the iPhone every few years later.

Along with Siri, the iPhone 4s also provided people with iOS 5 – Apple's own operating system, which introduced iCloud, Notification Center, iMessage, and many other notable features.

In September 2014, iPhone's first plus-size model was introduced, called iPhone 5. Two years later, Apple introduced two versions of the iPhone – 6 and 6s. The series continued, and two more iPhones were released: 7 and 7 Plus.

In September 2017, Apple introduced the 4K Apple TV, iPhone 8, and iPhone 8 Plus. Apple Watch Series 3 and iPhone X. Three new versions were introduced under iPhone X, including iPhone XS, iPhone XR, and iPhone XS Max.

In October 2020, the iPhone 12 series was introduced. It offered four phones in different colors, all of which had 5G support.

In September 2021, iPhone 13 and iPhone 13 Mini were introduced, along with iPhone 13 Pro and iPhone Pro Max. Apple recently leaked a video to give iPhone lovers a peek into what the iPhone 14 will look like and its features. Hint: It will be a *speed shock*.

Steve's Abandonment Issues

Steve's childhood was a happy one. He experienced life and the world in his own way. Despite knowing he was adopted, Steve became an outstanding guy. Besides his brash attitude and strange outbursts, Steve never showed any signs of abandonment issues.

In 1972, when Steve was about to finish his senior year at Homestead, he met Chrisann Brennan. Though she was the same age as him, she was still a junior. Her high cheekbones, green eyes, light brown hair, and fragile aura made her very attractive. She was going through her parent's divorce, which made her vulnerable.

After his graduation, Steve announced to his parents that he was moving into a cabin in Los Angeles with Chrisann. His parents were furious and strictly against it. They forbade him to do this but Steve simply said *goodbye* and walked out.

In Reed College, Chrisann would often come to meet him. By now, she was his on-and-off girlfriend. Their relationship sputtered erratically because he was more interested in his quest for enlightenment over putting down roots.

In 1977, when Steve was in the starting phase of making Apple computers, he reconnected with Chrisann. By now, he was living with Daniel Kottke in a 4-bedroom house. Once Chrisann moved in, their old relationship rekindled. It was during this time that Chrisann found out she was pregnant. Steve didn't take the news well.

Their relationship was an odd one from the start. Even though Chrisann had been someone else after their relationship strained, she still came back to him. Greg Calhoun, a friend from Reed and Chrisann's ex-boyfriend, visited them on Thanksgiving. When Chrisann gave him the news, Greg was happy, but he noticed Steve had distanced himself from the situation.

Steve had this tactic he used to isolate himself from a problem. He wasn't sure he was the father because even though Chrisann had been living with him, she had slept with other guys. However, Chrisann denied that she had been intimate with anyone after moving in. After much thinking, he concluded that either he could embrace parenthood or not. He decided to take refuge in the latter because he had other plans.

Steve knew that Chrisann was not the kind of girl who wanted marriage, so he advised her to get an abortion. However, Chrisann decided to keep the child. Steve was strongly against having the child because he did not want Chrisann to put the child up for adoption.

As Chrisann's pregnancy progressed, she became a little violent. However, her behavior change was mostly due to Steve's careless attitude. He often laughed at her during her tantrums, which enraged her more. Daniel was caught in the middle and was disturbed by the way things were progressing.

When Robert Friedland heard about Chrisann's pregnancy, he invited her to have the baby on the farm. A few days before the delivery, Steve flew to the farm to be with Chrisann. She moved into a small house with her daughter Lisa in Melon Park and decided not to sue Steve for child support. However, the County of San Mateo sued and intervened, and Steve was sent a notice. At first, Steve decided to fight the case but later agreed to take a paternity test.

Apple was about to go public and did not want any complications that might put him back in the back speed. The results showed a 94.41% chance Steve was the father. He was forced to pay $385 a month in child support.

It took Steve some time to wrap his head around the truth because he kept saying there was a high chance he was not the father.

Steve had abandoned Lisa, just like his birth parents had abandoned him. Even though he sent Chrisann more money for Lisa's school fee, he never used his visitation rights until years later.

Recalling his past in an interview, he said, *"I wish I had handled it differently. I could not see myself as a father then, so I didn't face up to it. But when the test results showed she was my daughter, it's not true that I doubted it. I agreed to support her until she was eighteen and give some money to Chrisann as well. I found a house in Palo Alto and fixed it up, and let them live there rent-free. Her mother found her great schools, which I paid for. I tried to do the right thing. But if I could do it over, I would do a better job."*

Despite his abandonment issues, he even named a computer Lisa. Some people think he did it because of his abandonment issues.

In 1989, Steve was giving a lecture at the Stanford Business School. He met his now-wife Lauren Powell there, who had recently graduated. After a quick conversation with Steve, Lauren left. When the lecture ended, Steve ran after her and convinced her to go on a date.

The Education Group was waiting for Steve to join them for dinner. Having the choice between them and Lauren, he ran back to her and asked if they could have dinner now, and she said "yes."

A few years later, at 36, Steve married Lauren, and they have two beautiful daughters.

The Death of a Genius

On October 5, 2011, the death of Steve Jobs rocked the world. He had fought a long battle with a rare type of pancreatic cancer. Some people believe that Steve would have lived past the age of 56 if he had received proper care.

He was first diagnosed with cancer in 2003. His doctors advised him to get surgery as soon as possible, but Steve delayed it for nine months. This might have been one reason that brought Steve closer to death.

When the doctors urged him to seek treatment, Steve flat out refused. He didn't want his body to be cut open. He felt that going under surgery would feel like a violation.

Jobs had always been a weird guy. Even his friend at college admitted that. An example of this is the time when his girlfriend revealed that she was pregnant. Despite the DNA test proving it was his child, Steve insisted it was very likely he wasn't the father.

When he got the news of his cancer, he leaned into the thinking that with a vegan diet, bowel cleansings, herbs, acupuncture, and other remedies, he could cure his disease. He even consulted a psychic to find out whether his disease would consume him or not.

Despite his unorthodox beliefs and unconventional practices, the cancer showed no signs of slowing down. In 2004, he finally agreed to get the surgery and revealed to his employees that he had undergone a tumor removal process.

Despite his reassurances to the employees, they could all see how Steve's health was deteriorating. In 2006, people showed concern for his health when he appeared at an Apple Conference looking weak and gaunt. His team reassured the public that Steve was as healthy as a horse.

In 2008, he once again appeared in an Apple event, and this time, he looked much weaker. By 2009, he wasn't giving keynote addresses. Apple downplayed his problems and said he simply had the "flu". As for Steve, he blamed hormone imbalance for his weight loss.

As time progressed, Steve could no longer deny that he was sick. He notified Apple employees through email that he was taking a couple of sick leaves.

In June 2009, The Wall Street Journal revealed that Steve had undergone a liver transplant. After six months, Steve was back at his desk. He was still struggling with his health but didn't want any more rumors to spread that he couldn't work any longer. In 2011, he took another leave and resigned as Apple's CEO by August. In a company email, he openly admitted that he no longer has the strength to look after such a huge empire.

Despite being sick, Steve stuck to his high standards. He changed 67 nurses until he found three he liked. After two months, the doctors gave up and said there was nothing more they could do.

On October 5, 2011, Steve Jobs passed away at his home, surrounded by family. Before dying, he agreed to get his biography penned, revealing that he took almost a year to get the surgery and the lengths he went to cure it by himself.

The Secrets Behind Steve Job's Success

There's no denying that Steve Jobs was a very successful man. He was not just a mind capable of coming up with innovative technology but also someone who grabbed opportunities with critical thinking.

Though his portfolio is not that long, an investment that pushed him into the billionaire club was Pixar. After his deal with Disney, he single-handedly became the person responsible for some of the most popular animated movies, such as Toy Story, Wall-E, and Finding Nemo.

People all over the world admire Steve Jobs for his bold vision. Entrepreneurs want to become like him so they can experience what life has to offer. Steve was a man of action and took risks only when he knew the outcome would be successful.

Many people believe that the only way to live life is to stand in the face of difficulty and say, "Not today!" However, what good will your hours of planning be if you make a mistake? Even after his death, Steve Jobs remains a role model to many entrepreneurs.

His advice has been immortalized on the Internet, serving as valuable advice for the next generations.

Steve Job's 10 Rules of Success

"I skate to where the puck is going to be, not where it has been."

Steve had a knack for predicting future trends. Call it his sixth sense or a habit of following the trends, but whatever it was, it allowed him to figure out what kind of innovation people would like in technology. While iPhones made a lasting impression, Apple's other inventions weren't far behind. iPod decreased the sales of CDs by introducing the iPod and the iTunes store.

To achieve a goal, you need to follow the trends. Think of it as a vision that you set for yourself. Where do you see yourself 5 years from now? For example, you are working as an employee at an IT company, but you hope to become an entrepreneur. So, you learn the skills necessary for being in the power seat.

This is how Steve came up with one invention after the other. Here's his advice on how you can become successful too:

Rule #1
Don't Have a Limited Mindset

"Things don't have to change the world to be important."

This might sound a bit contradictory, but the type of limited mindset that Steve talked about was the one you grew up with. You are told to follow certain rules as a young boy or girl because you need to fit in.

The average life cycle usually proceeds this way — work, get married, retire and live a happy life with your family. This limited mindset controls your creativity.

A simple fact is that people around you, who lack ambition, are no smarter than you. Once you understand this, your perception will change and open you up to new possibilities. Don't cast yourself into a mold because it will only stop you from achieving your goals.

Rule #2
Don't Sell Crap

"Details matter; it's worth waiting to get it right."

Perhaps the most important rule of success is never to sell crap; by that, we mean a bad product. You will find plenty of case studies online that will tell you how a company failed because of the founder's negligence.

Your only priority is to sell high-quality products because this will guarantee you make loyal customers. When your name is associated with trust, a brand becomes top of mind.

For example, you sell hair care products. They promise to offer strength, shine, and no split ends. However, the product fails to fulfill the promise. As a result, you lose customers. When you bring a new product on board, people are afraid to try it because of the bad press it receives. So, not only do you lose your old customers but any potential ones as well.

To prevent this scenario, you need to work on your brand and focus on the small details that make up your product.

Rule #3
Have Passion

"Love yourself and what you do – the only key to success."

A person working a 9 to 5 job will never be happy with their life if they don't get to do what they are passionate about. Let's say you had always dreamed about making a difference with your words. However, the only job you could get was in sales. The pay was good and at that time, you couldn't let the opportunity pass. Fast forward a few years and you are stuck.

Is this the kind of life you want to lead? Yes, it can be tough to follow your passion but you know what they say, "The fruit of passion tastes sweet."

All your struggles will be worth the wait when you finally feel happy doing what you love.

Rule #4
Be Your Own Designer

"Don't let the noise of other people's opinions drown out your own inner voice."

Woz and Steve designed the first Apple computer on their own because they did not have the money to purchase a computer kit. Everyone wanted it when they showed the design to others in the Homebrew Computer Club. That's how Steve knew he was doing something right.

Never let other people decide for you. Drown out the noise of their opinions with your inner voice by saying, "I can do it."

It's a cliché but one that works!

Design for yourself, and don't give anyone a second thought. The moment you do, you will regret your decision later in life.

Rule #5
Gather a Team With Great People

"When you're in a startup, the first ten people will determine whether the company succeeds or not."

As an entrepreneur, it's alright to admit you cannot do everything on your own. One job that falls on your shoulder, which might seem like a burden at first but will give you immense relief is recruitment.

You don't need to hire a seasoned professional. Just be someone who's great at something. These people are self-made and don't require any management.

This helps you in numerous ways. For example, a wet behind the ears recruit will need to be trained, which will take your time and money. On the other hand, an expert will know exactly what to do after a simple explanation.

This is where leadership comes in. Your recruits need to share your vision so they can understand what you are aiming for and can work towards that goal.

Rule #6
Don't Make It About the Money

"The journey is the reward."

Steve Jobs was a millionaire by the time he turned 23. As he got older, the millions kept adding until he finally reached billionaire status. However, according to Steve, money wasn't why he founded Apple.

Yes, money certainly makes life easy. It allows you to do things you had only dreamt about. You can invest in ideas with short-term payback, and that's about it. For Steve, what mattered more was the company he had created from the ground up, the people he employed, and the products he was selling.

"Be like Steve Jobs." If a meme badly needed creating, it would be this one of entrepreneurs.

"The only way to do great work is to love what you do."

The purpose of a company is to offer an exceptional product or service. It should be different from others and fulfill their needs. Not only this, but you should be proud to sell this product. Your family and friends should recommend it.

Steve understood this concept pretty well. He believed that it would likely fail if you didn't have faith in your product. Having a successful line of products such as iPhone, iPads, and more, Steve was as proud as a CEO could be.

Today, Apple is one of the most successful companies in the world. As an innovator, you must be creative and see beyond the pre-existing life patterns.

This will allow you to spot an opening in the market where you can make your mark. Think about it: You wouldn't invest your time and money into making something worthless, right? A product sells more because its creator believes they have created something of high quality.

So, you need to focus not only on the conception of your product but also on its manufacturing. While running your business, you will face some unethical tactics that will tempt you to take a route that will give you a great product but stop you from being honest to your customers.

The opinions of those who are close to you matter the most. Since they can be sincere, they will give you an unbiased review. Their feedback is what helps you make your product's success more achievable.

Rule #8
Build Around Customers

"You can't look at the competition and say you're going to do it better. You have to look at the competition and say you're going to do it differently."

When World War II ended, people went through a tough time. The war had ravaged many countries. As a result, some materials couldn't be found, creating difficulty in making products. Many companies shut down, and because of this, people had no choice but to buy whatever they were offering.

The number of companies started to grow gradually as time passed, forcing existing companies to change strategies and improve their products.

The point of telling you this story is that for a long time, companies were focused on making a better product than their competitors, and in this race, they forgot to factor in the needs and wants of customers.

Hence, today, you will find numerous products in the market that serve the same purpose but are slightly different in design.

The key to creating a successful product is to adjust and improve constantly. Apple's success is due to its unique features that appeal to high-end clients. Yes, the products are expensive, but people understand their value and are willing to pay a high price to get their hands on an iPhone.

Apple prides itself on offering its customers reliable and friendly customer service. Loyalty helps build a brand and convince customers they will get more value when choosing them over competitors. During an Apple conference, an audience member accused Steve of not paying attention to its products.

To this, Steve replied, "You can please some of the people some of the time. One of the things I've always known is that you've got to start with the customer experience and work your way backwards to the technology."

The customer is not always right, but the customer always comes first. So, pay attention to the needs and wants of customers and work on their feedback to show them their voice is heard.

Rule #9
Marketing Helps Create Value

"A lot of times, people don't know what they want until you show it to them."

A customer is standing in a store's aisle for hair care products. Your brand is right in the middle and is surrounded by six competitors. After giving all the brands much thought, the customer picks up your competitor's product.

The reason?

Well, there are many, but at the core is marketing. Marketing helps your customers see your product's actual value.

Apple gained immense popularity because of the way Steve demonstrated its features at the reveal conference. This is why a company should focus on building its brand image rather than beating the competition.

When talking about values, there are many things to consider. Apart from coming up with a unique product, you must also invest in it from time to time to retain its vitality and relevance.

So, develop a core value and then create your marketing campaign based on it. This will show your customers that you believe in a cause and are not just selling your product to make money.

Rule #10
Stay Hungry, Stay Foolish

"Have the courage to follow your heart and intuition. They somehow know what you truly want to become."

Perseverance separates successful entrepreneurs from those who have experienced failure a lot.

Steve's last rule is that you will be more willing to work more if you are satisfied with what you have created so far. The important thing is never to let hunger die or be afraid of change.

Staying foolish does not mean you make mistakes. It simply means that you continue to follow your wild and silly dreams.

You have probably heard this a dozen times — success comes to those who work hard. Steve always talked fondly about the time he dropped out of college. He naively chose a college as expensive as Stanford and burdened his middle-class parents with paying the tuition.

After a while, he didn't see any value in studying because it didn't align with what he had in mind. But he doesn't regret dropping out of college because Apple would have never been born if he hadn't.

No matter what you do in life, make sure you are passionate about it. Tenacity and perseverance lead you to success, so don't give up on your dreams until you are entirely sure they are unachievable. Even then, come up with a new plan to fulfill your dreams.

Imagine living in a world without Steve Jobs. You wouldn't have iPhones, MacBooks, iPods, Apple Watches, or iPads. Though his technology made billions of dollars, he also inspired countless entrepreneurs and showed them the path to success.

Just like Mark Zuckerberg, Oprah Winfrey, and Bill Gates, he made his own rules and never paid attention to the opinions of others.

Steve Job's Advice for Entrepreneurs

Steve Jobs changed the world with his revolutionary thinking and technology. His attempt at revamping the mobile phone market allowed him to become a billionaire. Though he is no longer amongst us, his advice still lives on.

His creative mind made him an idol of entrepreneurs all over the world. They found his advice inspiring, like a bright light that guided them through a dark tunnel. He had much more to share with us but was sadly taken away too soon.

However, his words made a lasting impression. Following is his advice for entrepreneurs who are just starting or struggling to make it.

Be and Don't Be Passionate About What You Do

Passion is the one thing that keeps you interested in what you do. However, your passion is a hobby, and when you start to make a career out of it, it becomes work.

Steve never said that you should turn your passion into a business idea. However, he did say, "The most important thing is being passionate about what you are doing."

Did you spot the slight change in words? It's not "do what you love" but "love what you do." Steve was never interested in technology. Yes, he had a knack for it, but spirituality was what he pursued religiously. It wasn't until he and Woz created the first Apple computer that he came to love what he knew of. So, instead of monetizing your passion, monetize your skills. Ultimately, you will become passionate about what you are doing.

Stay Focused

Focus was the one trait ingrained in Steve's personality, which he had honed on his trip to India and through Zen training. He filtered out all the advice that he considered distractions. His family members and colleagues often would get exasperated by his attitude when trying to get his attention for a legal matter or medical diagnosis. He would stay in his zone, give the person a cold stare, and then go back to work.

When Steve was on his deathbed, Larry Page (to-be CEO of Google) paid him a visit. Even though Apple and Google had been battling, Steve was willing to give Larry some advice.

He asked Larry about the products that Google was focusing on. Steve told him to single out five of them and eliminate the rest.

"Unimportant products drag you down and will turn you into Microsoft. Their strategy is to roll out one product after the other. They are adequate but don't have any value."

Larry followed Steve's advice and told his employees to focus their time and energy on Google+ and Android and make them as beautiful as Steve would have.

Staying focused is not just about paying attention to your business. It's also about adopting a positive attitude. Though Steve had many negative habits as a teenager, he still had focus. Being adopted would have made him cynical, but he chose to see the positive side of it. He got loving parents who were willing to go to great lengths to make him happy. From a young age, Steve had been interested in computers and technology. He sharpened his skills and achieved his dreams in adulthood.

That's the type of energy you should carry in life. The more good you feel about yourself, the better you will be able to work on your goals. Fail Forward.

Failure is a part of success. The way you choose to respond to these failures is what makes a difference. Steve was fired from Apple in 1984. The reason was that his latest creation Macintosh was priced too high, and no one could afford it. As mentioned earlier, the product was not at fault, but its marketing.

In 2005, he gave a commencement speech at Stanford, discussing the incident.

"I didn't see it then, but it turned out that getting fired from Apple was the best thing that could have ever happened to me. The heaviness of being successful was replaced by the lightness of being a beginner again, less sure about everything. It freed me to enter one of the most creative periods of my life."

What does this teach us?

Never fear failure! It's the one thing that opens up more opportunities for you and allows you to improve yourself.

Take Risks

Ask any successful CEO, and they will tell you that taking risks is a part of running any business. Steve came up with one great invention after the other. When the iPod was introduced, iPhone sales went down, which was Apple's most prized product. However, this didn't stop him.

He came up with more new designs and knew that the iPhone would retake the throne, which eventually happened.

Let Time Limit You

Here's a formula that Steve created just for entrepreneurs.

"Remembering that I'll be dead soon is the most important tool I've ever encountered to help me make the big choices in life. Because almost everything — all external expectations, all pride, all fear of embarrassment or failure – these things just fall away in the face of death, leaving only what is truly important."

Sometimes, you need a push to do what you have been thinking about. It's neither procrastination nor fear but simply a mindset that convinces you that you have time.

Remember: Time is limited. Steve says not to get trapped by dogma. This will make you live a life based on what other people think, which is not at all productive for your business. Follow your intuition because it will get you to the point you want to reach.

When Behind, Leapfrog

From the start, we have thought that a company is considered innovative when it comes up with unique and new ideas one after the other. What happens when this company falls behind?

It gives you something to think about.

When Steve created iMac, he was focused on offering users ease in managing their videos and photos. What he forgot was adding an option for downloading music.

People who had PCs were burning CDs then. This lack of features in iMac didn't go down well with them. Steve couldn't believe he and his team had missed such an obvious thing.

He had to do something to right this wrong. Instead of upgrading the iMac, he devised a system that changed the music industry. He created the iPod, iTunes, and the iTunes Store. The iPod quickly became a huge success, which got Steve a little worried.

He was happy with the success of his new creation but feared that something might endanger it. So, he cannibalized the product and introduced new versions of the iPhone.

This story teaches us that never stop inventing when you have a winning product.

Opportunities Are Often Disguised As Obstacles

When Steve and Woz were developing their first computer, they ran out of money. They believed in their idea so much that they decided to make a few sacrifices. Woz sold his calculator and Steve his van.

Their efforts paid off because people were highly impressed when they first displayed their invention.

Creativity comes in two ways: By connecting with people and things. Your life experiences allow you to see things that people usually miss. For example, Steve took calligraphy classes, which were useless until he created the Macintosh. He studied hospitality and design, which allowed him to connect different ideas.

The more you experience – personally and vicariously – the richer your life becomes. You get this sixth sense, which allows you to make a connection between things. However, simplicity should not be forgotten.

Think like a child. When they discover new things, their favorite word is "Why." Strip away your assumptions and preconceptions about how things work.

Just because you add a simple feature to your invention doesn't mean you can make it complex. Sometimes, it's about walking the fine line between just right and not quite right.

There's a famous story about Steve and when he held the first iPod.

Weighing the iPhone in his hand, Steve takes the headphones and inserts the jack into the iPod. Engineers who worked on the device stand in silence. Steve doesn't press the play button, and his brows furrow. Something is wrong.

He takes out the jack and inserts it back into the iPod. He does this multiple times, panicking the engineers. The launch is just a few days away, and the engineers don't know if they will be able to make any changes. Suddenly, Steve says, "Where's the click?"

An exhausted engineer asks, "Click?"

Steve says, "People need to hear a click when the jack is inserted. Without it, they will have no idea whether the headphones are working or not. They will keep inserting and taking out the jack until the headphones break. This is not an elegant solution."

It was a simple click, yet no one noticed. Only Steve was able to make the connection.

When people notice such clicks, their innovation level increases, allowing them to develop a successful product.

Let Curiosity Lead You

Have you ever gone with your gut? Curiosity killed the cat, but according to Steve, it leads you to success. During his career, he followed this philosophy till the very end.

Steve illustrated this point in his speech at Stanford by telling the audience that when he dropped out of Reed, he had the freedom to do whatever he wanted. So, he took the classes that piqued his interest. One of them was calligraphy, which he found fascinating.

Though the course had no practical purpose for where Steve was headed at the time, it later came to his rescue when he was designing the Macintosh. It gave him an understanding of typography, which helped set the fonts.

Steve believed that intuition and curiosity are trustworthy guides. Even when you can't see what the outcome of your decision might be, you still should have faith in it.

Say "No" to Things

Saying "yes" to things can be difficult when all you want to do is say no. However, in business, when you brainstorm ideas and come up with a dozen, you find it hard to scratch some when all of them are really good.

When Steve was fired, he was free to work on some of his ideas that he wouldn't have, had he been at Apple. When Apple rehired him, the company was working on a total of 350 products. It was pure chaos.

After evaluating the products, he decided to stick with 10 in 2 years. He then created several A-Teams and assigned each a product.

It's possible that he could have scratched some great products, but by focusing on the ones he could predict would become successful, he could roll out some fantastic products.

Master the Message

Why did the Macintosh fail? It's because no one paid attention to its marketing. As a result, no research was done on the target market, leading to a hefty price tag. As a result, no one bought it. That's what got Steve fired from Apple.

It wasn't his fault, but he missed one significant element of running a business. Though Steve says that the time apart from Apple gave him a new perspective to approach things, he was still hurt when someone he hired took over his position.

Let's say you have a great idea. You are 100% sure that people will love your product. However, once it's on the market, you don't receive the type of response you had hoped for. So, where did you go wrong?

Your message wasn't clear!

After the Macintosh incident, Steve became one of the best corporate storytellers in the world. To this date, people still watch his iPhone reveal video.

So, when introducing your product to the public, don't make it a presentation. Tell the tale of how it was formed and how it will benefit the buyer.

Conclusion

The Legacy of the Tech Titan

To this day, the speech Steve gave in 2007 when revealing the first iPhone is considered by many as one of the best product reveals. Though he passed away too soon, his legacy lived on.

Steve was not just a name. He had become a brand that created Apple. In 2018, more than 2 billion iPhones were sold, changing the way people communicate with each other.

After Steve's death, Woz said in an interview that he would always remember his friend as a person who was very quick of mind. Woz added that whenever he and Steve talked about something, he was always right.

We can all agree that Steve's vision for Apple gave new meaning to the world of technology. Steve had created the iPad without any market research because he was confident, excited, and persistent in his ideas.

Despite his brilliant mind, what got to him, in the end, were his personal beliefs. Many doctors revealed that Steve's pancreatic cancer was treatable.

Steve had left any thoughts of his company behind on his deathbed. His focus was now on the afterlife instead. He would often say that he was 50-50 on the existence of God. He told Walter Isaacson, the American author who wrote his biography, that not knowing whether there is a god or not is a mystery that no one will be able to solve.

He then said something profound that would give people a glimpse into Steve's mind —*"I like to believe that the wisdom you've accumulated, somehow it lives on."*

"Sometimes, I think it's just like an On-Off switch. Click. And you're gone. That's why I don't like putting On-Off switches on Apple devices."

Steve was a man with a vision. He never did anything half-assed. In the beginning, he did face some challenges, but they were faced with confidence.

One thing Steve stressed on at numerous times is having a team of people you can trust. He had Woz, and without him, Apple would have never been born.

He surrounded himself with competent people and ensured they had the same vision as him. Like other geniuses, such as Elon Musk, Richard Branson, and Jeff Bezos, Steve also started from scratch and built an empire he was proud of.

A piece of advice for entrepreneurs that stick home was:

"For the past 33 years, I have looked in the mirror every morning and asked myself: 'If today were the last day of my life, would I want to do what I am about to do today?' And whenever the answer has been 'No' for too many days in a row, I know I need to change something."

Never get stuck in a rut! We are not saying that you should spend your last day on earth relaxing or making 13 tapes but do something that will make you happy.

Even on his deathbed, Steve gave Larry Page advice on how he could make his company succeed. That's the true mark of a successful entrepreneur.

So, stay focused and take risks. Do not let time limit you because it will be the death of your creativity. Opportunities often come disguised as obstacles. So, if you are sure your idea will be successful, go to great lengths to turn it into reality.

Marketing is a vital part of every business. It's what can make or break your brand. Steve learned this the hard way, but the break he got from responsibilities was a welcome change for him.

Lastly, let curiosity lead you because it might have killed the cat, but you know better. Listen closely to make connections because it's the key to creating a brand that customers will not only love but advocate for fiercely.

Disclaimer

www.ingramcontent.com/pod-product-compliance
Lightning Source LLC
LaVergne TN
LVHW041800190726
843493LV00008B/2709